monday morning®

LANGUAGE BOOSTERS

By Dana McMillan

Illustrated by Corbin Hillam

Publisher: Roberta Suid
Editor: Mary McClellan
Cover design: David Hale
Design and production: Susan Pinkerton

m nday morning®

Monday Morning is a registered trademark of
Monday Morning Books, Inc.

ISBN 0-912107-83-9

Printed in the United States of America
9 8 7 6 5 4 3 2 1

Contents

Introduction   4

Card and Board Games   5
  Antonym Bingo (antonyms)   6
  Sentence Tic-Tac-Toe (parts of speech)   8
  Look All Ways (sentence construction)   10
  Compound Word Concentration
    (compound words)   12
  Direction Please (dictionary skills)   14
  Blends Obstacle Course (blends)   16

Game Shows   17
  Mystery Phrases (word phrases)   18
  Synonyms Game (synonyms)   20
  Kid's Court (creative writing)   22
  Occupations (questioning skills)   24
  Truthful Story (creative writing)   26
  Famous People Jeopardy (memory)   27
  Picture Charades
    (nonverbal communication)   28

Words in Action   29
  Rhyming Categories (rhyming words)   30
  Punctuation Emphasis (punctuation)   32
  Beautiful Mixup (descriptive words)   34
  Adverb Reaction (adverbs)   35
  Stump the Leader (questioning skills)   36
  Dare to Do It (creative thinking)   37
  Vowel Charades (vowel sounds)   38

Word Challenges   39
  Radio Show (creative writing)   40
  ABC Game (beginning sounds)   42
  Souped-Up Words (spelling)   43
  Alphabet Poetry (poetry writing)   44
  Cause and Effect Toss
    (cause and effect sentences)   45
  Bean Sounds (beginning,
    middle, and ending sounds)   46
  Dictionary (word meanings)   47
  Headlines (story content)   48

Team Games   49
  Comparisons (creative thinking)   50
  From Here to There (opposites)   52
  City Scramble (alphabet)   54
  Next Letter Please (alphabetical order)   55
  How to Do It (descriptive writing)   56

Visual Activities   57
  License Plates (creative writing)   58
  Letter Shift (spelling)   60
  Prefix and Suffix Flip Book
    (prefixes and suffixes)   61
  Picture Puzzles (visual memory)   62
  Comic Strip Stories (creative writing)   63
  Vocabulary Ladder (vocabulary)   64

Introduction

The activities in *Language Boosters* are based on ideas that developed in workshops for teachers. Through the years, the Learning Exchange, a nonprofit educational resource center, has offered workshops that help teachers look for creative, hands-on methods to teach skills to children. *Language Boosters* activities help children learn traditional language skills in an involving, interactive way.

Teachers, parents, or youth-group leaders will all find activities that appeal to their children. Many of the games are designed to be used with a group of any size. Some are appropriate for a family to play.

The activities in *Language Boosters* are grouped according to the style of game. For example, one section of the book contains activities based on familiar game shows. These will be fun for small groups, with adult supervision provided as necessary. Adapt the activities according to the skills of the children playing. You may want to be the game leader for some of them that require adult assistance. For older children, pick a game leader from the group. Some of the activities will work well in a language learning center in the classroom.

Any of the activities requiring materials list ones that are inexpensive and easy to find. You can also make substitutions when necessary. For example, if the activity calls for index cards, you could cut game cards from sheets of construction paper.

I hope that you and your children find these language activities stimulating and that you find many opportunities for fun language experiences.

Dana McMillan
The Learning Exchange
2720 Walnut
Kansas City, MO 64108

CARD AND BOARD GAMES

Antonym Bingo

A variation on Bingo offers practice in recognizing antonyms.

MATERIALS:
Oaktag
Scissors
Marker or pen
Index cards
Chips

PLAYERS:
Game leader
4 to 30

PREPARATION:
1. Cut game boards from the oaktag.
2. Divide the game boards into 20 equal squares.
3. Print the first words of the Antonym Pairs on the game boards. Be sure to make each board different.
4. Print the second words of the Antonym Pairs on index cards.

ACTIVITY:
1. Have each player select a game board and ten chips.
2. The game leader then reads a word from the deck of index cards. The players look on their game boards for the matching antonyms. If they find a match, they cover the word with a chip.
3. The first player to cover a row horizontally, diagonally, or vertically should call out "Antonym Bingo!"
4. The game leader checks the words covered on the game board against those called during the game. If the antonyms match, the player wins and becomes the leader for the next round. Players may change their boards for each new round.

Antonym Pairs

accept/deny
add/subtract
adult/child
advance/retreat
after/before
bad/good
busy/idle
buy/sell
calm/excited
chilly/warm
combine/separate
courage/cowardice
dark/light
decrease/increase
destroy/build
early/late
fake/genuine
friend/enemy
help/hinder

individual/group
love/hate
more/less
obey/disobey
open/close
polite/rude
rear/front
receive/give
rich/poor
save/spend
sick/well
slow/quick
strength/weakness
sunrise/sunset
tall/short
top/bottom
victory/defeat
young/old

Sentence Tic-Tac-Toe

Play tic-tac-toe and practice the parts of speech.

MATERIALS:
Strips of paper
Marker
Chalkboard and chalk

PLAYERS:
Game leader
6 to 20 players

PREPARATION:
1. Print sentences on strips of paper, underlining one word in each sentence. (See the Sentence List.) Make a master list of the sentences, with the part of speech written in parentheses.
2. Draw a tic-tac-toe grid on the chalkboard.

ACTIVITY:
1. Players divide into two teams. One team is the X team and the other one is the O team.
2. One player from a team draws a sentence strip.
3. The player reads the sentence aloud and names the part of speech for the underlined word. The game leader checks the master list to see if the player is correct.
4. If the player is correct, he or she puts an X or an O on a square of the grid. If the player is incorrect, the team doesn't get to mark a space on the grid.
5. The first player of the next team then draws a sentence strip. Play continues until one team has made tic-tac-toe.

Sentence List

1. The trapeze artist <u>swung</u> back and forth. (verb)
2. You can make a <u>beautiful</u> bowl. (adjective)
3. Your best <u>friend</u> will like it. (noun)
4. Carrie is the <u>best</u> pitcher on the team. (adjective)
5. A sea otter floats <u>peacefully</u>. (adverb)
6. The clanging <u>alarm</u> woke me up. (noun)
7. Six acrobats <u>tumbled</u> across the stage. (verb)
8. I drank a glass of cool <u>water</u>. (noun)
9. Rory ran <u>quickly</u> through the field. (adverb)
10. Trish squeezed the <u>juicy</u> orange. (adjective)
11. Two machines are <u>slowly</u> moving the earth. (adverb)
12. Gary's parents <u>try</u> to conserve energy. (verb)
13. <u>Maria</u> caught the ball. (proper noun)
14. Their instruments <u>are</u> homemade. (verb)
15. Jupiter is the <u>biggest</u> of all the planets. (adjective)
16. Very hot volcanos formed the <u>Hawaiian Islands</u>. (proper noun)
17. A pigeon can fly <u>farther</u> than a parakeet. (adverb)
18. I <u>made</u> a color wheel from a paper plate. (verb)
19. The <u>cat</u> looked out the window. (noun)
20. The <u>hungry</u> man knocked at the door. (adjective)

Look All Ways

Try this game of combining phrases to make sentences.

MATERIALS:
Different colors of construction paper
Scissors
Marker
Envelope
Paper
Pencils

PLAYERS:
3 to 6 players

PREPARATION:
1. Cut the construction paper into playing cards.
2. Use one color for each sentence. Print a phrase from the sentence on each card. (See the Sentence List.)
3. Print the rules on the front of the envelope, and store the cards in the envelope when they are not in use.

ACTIVITY:
1. Each player needs paper and pencil. The dealer sorts the cards into color groups and deals a color group to each player, facedown.
2. When all of the cards have been dealt, the players may look at their cards and arrange them to form sentences.
3. The players write down the sentences they have formed.
4. The players then look for another combination of phrases that will form sentences from their sets of cards. All sentences should be written down.
5. When the players have written as many sentences as they can, they draw new sets of cards or exchange sets and follow the same procedure.
6. The player who forms the most sentences wins.

Sentence List

1. the brown leaves/fell/to the ground/yesterday/because it was windy
2. last Sunday/Mom took us/to the park/because it was a warm, sunny day
3. last week/while skiing/in Vermont/Tom broke his arm
4. today/I rode my bike/to school/so I wouldn't be late
5. if I had/a lot of money/and/my own car/I'd take a trip to Disneyland
6. she swam/across the pool/in thirty seconds/while competing in a race
7. someday/I would like to become/a doctor/so I could help people
8. we could/form a baseball club/if people were interested/and /sell cards
9. once/we went/to the zoo/to see the animals/and/it rained
10. Saturday/we will go/to the football game/with friends

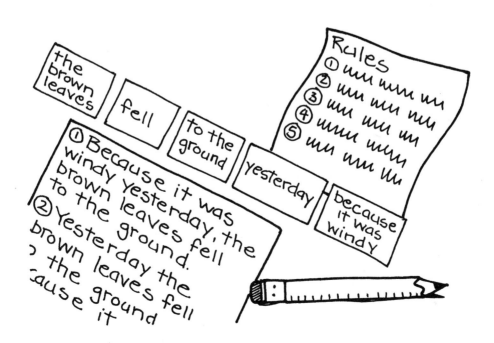

Compound Word Concentration

Players look for compound word combinations.

MATERIALS:
Index cards
Marker

PLAYERS:
2 to 6 players

PREPARATION:
Write parts of compound words on index cards. (See the Word List.)

ACTIVITY:
1. Shuffle the cards, and place them facedown in rows on a table or the floor.
2. In turn, each player turns over two cards and reads them aloud.
3. If the cards form a compound word, the player has made a pair and removes them. If the cards don't form a compound, the player turns them facedown again.
4. When all of the cards have been matched, the winner is the player with the most cards.

Word List

foot	ball	rain	coat	rail	road
sun	shine	class	room	play	time
green	house	brief	case	work	bench
sail	boat	eye	brow	ground	hog
tight	rope	ply	wood	card	board
butter	cup	mail	bag	home	work

Direction Please

Practice alphabetizing with this dictionary game.

MATERIALS:
Strips of paper
Marker
Index cards
Paper clips
File folder

PREPARATION:
1. Print the guide words listed on the ends of the sentence strips.
2. Print the word sets on index cards. A different color of index card can be used for each set of words.
3. Clip each set together.
4. Make a copy of the list of words with the arrows indicating where the words fall in each set. Put the copy in the folder for self-checking.

ACTIVITY:
1. A player works with one set of guide words and cards at a time.
2. The player figures out where the words would fall and places the cards below the guide words strip in the following manner:
   • If the word comes before the guide words, put the card to the left of the strip.
   • If the word comes after the guide words, put the card to the right of the strip.
   • If the word falls between the guide words, put the card below the strip.
3. After placing the cards where they belong, the player checks their placement with the list in the folder.

Guide Words and Word Sets

angled—animal husbandry

anguish▽

androgen◇

annul◇

annex◇

anglo▽

drag—drawback

draggle▽

drench◇

dragonfly▽

doll◇

dream◇

hidebound—high tide

hipped◇

hierodule▽

herse◇

highday▽

hill◇

jester—job

jet▽

jewel▽

javelin◇

junior◇

jack◇

pipeline—pitch

pitcher◇

pinch◇

pita▽

plash◇

pit▽

refinement—refuse

real◇

reflow▽

remember◇

refrain▽

refer◇

strontic—study

stroud▽

subsonic◇

streak◇

strudel▽

string◇

tule—tupi

turkey◇

tunic▽

trunk◇

tup▽

tweed◇

Blends Obstacle Course

Use this game for practice in blends.

MATERIALS:
Poster board
Marker
Peel-off dots
Spinner or die
Game pawns

PLAYERS:
2 to 4 players

PREPARATION:
1. Print "Blends Obstacle Course" at the top of the poster board.
2. Use the peel-off dots to form a track on the board.
3. Print "Start" next to the first dot and "Finish" next to the last dot.
4. Print blends on the other dots: sp, gr, st, fl, cr, bl, cl.
5. To make the game more challenging, write special directions next to some of the dots: move ahead 1 space, move ahead 2 spaces, move back 1 space, lose a turn, take another turn.

ACTIVITY:
1. Roll the die or spin to see who goes first.
2. Each player rolls the die or spins and moves the number of spaces indicated.
3. To stay on the space, the player must say a word that starts with the blend. For example, a player who lands on the "bl" space might say "blue."
4. Words may not be repeated during the game. A player who repeats a word or cannot name a blend word goes back to start.
5. The first player to finish is the winner.

GAME SHOWS

Mystery Phrases

Players guess letters to fill in the blanks of a mystery phrase.

MATERIALS:
Chalkboard
Chalk
Watch or clock with second hand

PLAYERS:
Game leader
Letter person
3 players

ACTIVITY:
1. The players sit facing the chalkboard. The game leader and letter person stand in front of the board.
2. The game leader and letter person choose a phrase to be used in the first round. (See the Phrase List.) The letter person draws lines on the board to indicate the letters in each word of the phrase. For example, "odd man out" would be indicated by

— — —   — — —   — — —.

3. The game leader then calls on the first player to guess one of the letters used in the phrase. If the guess is correct, the letter person fills in any of the blanks where the letter appears in the phrase. For example, if the player guesses "d," the blanks on the board would look like this: __dd   __ __ __   __ __ __.
4. The player is then given ten seconds to guess the phrase. If the player can't guess the phrase, the next player takes a turn. If the player picks a letter that isn't in the phrase, the letter person writes it next to the blanks, and the next player takes a turn.
5. The player who guesses the phrase correctly wins for that round and earns 5 points for each letter in the phrase. After three rounds, the scores are added and the winner may choose to become the game leader or the letter person for the next round.

Phrase List

hit the jackpot

odd man out

a happy medium

out of this world

hold your horses

making ends meet

all keyed up

shoot for the stars

better safe than sorry

that's the way the cookie crumbles

get the picture

top of the line

make a beeline

don't jump to conclusions

if the shoe fits wear it

no end in sight

when the going gets tough the tough get going

one good turn deserves another

Synonyms Game

Try this synonyms version of Password.

MATERIALS:
Index cards
Marker

PLAYERS:
Game leader
4 players

PREPARATION:
Print words from the Word List on index cards. Make two cards for each word.

ACTIVITY:
1. Each team has two players. The game leader keeps track of the cards.
2. The game leader gives the same word to a member on each team.
3. The player on one team gives his or her partner a synonym for the word on the card. If the partner doesn't guess correctly, the player on the other team gives another synonym. The teams take turns until someone guesses the word on the card.
4. After the word has been guessed, the game leader gives the other partners a new word card.
5. The team that guesses the word first gets 1 point. The first team to reach 10 points wins. Switch positions for a new game.

Word List

absurd	legend
active	lovely
adore	mad
affection	mysterious
anxious	noisy
battle	odd
bold	ordinary
break	patient
calm	peaceful
champion	plain
cheap	polite
chilly	powerful
cruel	pretty
delicate	rough
depart	secret
different	shelter
disaster	sloppy
evil	smooth
false	strange
fall	take
gently	tidy
great	trouble
happy	tough
huge	unkind
intelligent	vicious
joy	warm
kind	weird
laugh	young

Kid's Court

Make up cases to take to court.

MATERIALS:
Black trash bag
Scissors
White paper
Gavel
Writing paper
Pencils

PLAYERS:
6 to 30 players

PREPARATION:
1. Make a judge's robe out of the trash bag. Cut a slit in the bottom of the bag for the head and in the sides for the arms.
2. Make a collar from the white paper.

ACTIVITY:
1. Divide the players into three teams. Each team should have pencils and paper.
2. Each team writes two or three cases to be heard in a small claims court. For example, the cases could involve something that was borrowed and not returned or a promise that was made and not kept.
3. When the cases are completed, pick a case to be heard in court. The team whose case was picked has the choice of defendant or plaintiff and chooses a team member to represent them. The second team chooses a member to take the other role, and the third team chooses a member to be the judge for the case.
4. The teams are given five minutes to discuss their positions. The judge's team may help with questions to ask both parties.
5. The judge sits at a table in the center of the room, wearing the robe. The defendant and the plaintiff sit on opposite sides of the judge, with their team members behind them.
6. One person from any team is the bailiff, asking the people to rise when the judge enters the court and asking the parties to promise to tell the truth.

7. The judge asks questions of both parties to help determine the sequence of events, the value of the property, and any other evidence that will help the judge to make a decision.

8. After listening to the answers, the judge makes a fair decision, based on the evidence. The judge can also decide if any money should be awarded to either party.

9. The team that wins the case gets 10 points. After hearing cases from each team, the one with the most points wins.

Sample Court Case

Case: Johnson vs. Patterson

Defendant: Cara Patterson

Plaintiff: Jason Johnson

Claim:
Jason Johnson claims that Cara Patterson borrowed his bike for her paper route and had an accident which resulted in $55 in damages to the bike.

Defendant's Defense:
Cara Patterson has stated that Jason's bike was not in good working order when she borrowed it and that the brakes failed, causing her to be unable to stop when she was traveling down a steep hill.

Amount of the Suit:
$55 to pay the repair bill for the bike.

Occupations

Players try to guess the occupation without the most common words as clues.

MATERIALS:
Paper and pencil for each player
Chalk and chalkboard

PLAYERS:
5 or more players

ACTIVITY:
1. Each player writes a common occupation at the top of the paper. (See the Occupations List.) Below the occupation, the player writes five words commonly associated with the occupation. For example, if the occupation were teacher, the player might write the following words: children, books, chalkboard, classroom, grades.
2. The first player chosen is the Occupation Person. The Occupation Person picks someone to be the Interviewer.
3. The Interviewer uses the Occupation Person's list to ask questions, without using any of the words on the list. For example, the Interviewer could ask, "Do you work during the summer?" or "Do you read stories to young people?" The Interviewer could not ask, "Do you work with children?" or "Do you read books?"
4. The other players try to guess the occupation from the questions and answers. The first player to guess becomes the next Occupation Person.

Occupations List

surgeon
architect
dentist
secretary
banker
waiter
mail carrier
nurse
truck driver
artist
musician
veterinarian
grocery clerk

computer operator
firefighter
author
construction worker
police officer
doctor
homemaker
principal
pilot
astronaut
movie star
reporter
cook

Truthful Story

Find the author of a story in a group of possible pretenders.

MATERIALS:
Paper
Pencils
Large, numbered cards (1-20)

PLAYERS:
Game leader
6 to 30 players

PREPARATION:
Each player writes a story about something that really happened. It can be about something that happened to the player recently or a long time ago. The story should contain as many facts as possible.

ACTIVITY:
1. The game leader chooses three players. The players go out of the room with the leader, who picks one of the three stories to use. The three players go over the story until they are familiar enough with it to pretend it happened to them.
2. When the three players return to the room, they sit in front of the group.
3. The game leader reads the story aloud. The game leader then picks people to ask panel members questions. The panel members try to convince the group that they are telling the truth. The game leader turns over the number cards to remind the group of how many questions are left.
4. After 20 questions have been asked, the group votes on who wrote the story.
5. When the voting is over, the group leader asks the player who wrote the story to stand up.
6. The game may continue with a new story and new panel members.

Famous People Jeopardy

Players use clues to name a famous person.

MATERIALS:
Index cards
Marker
Paper
Pencil
Bulletin board
Pushpins

PLAYERS:
Game leader
2 to 3 players

PREPARATION:
1. Choose 20 famous people and write a fact about each one on the front of the index card. Write the person's name on the back of the card.
2. Assign each card a point value, according to its difficulty. For example, a well-known fact about George Washington might have a value of 5 points. A fact about Amelia Earhart might be worth 20 points.
3. Make a list of the famous people and their facts for the game leader to use to check the answers.
4. Pin the cards on the bulletin board in rows according to their point values.

ACTIVITY:
1. The players sit in front of the bulletin board.
2. The game leader calls on a player to begin. The player picks a card under the point value he or she would like to attempt.
3. The game leader reads the fact on the card, and the player tries to name the famous person.
4. If the player is correct, the game leader takes down the card and gives it to the player.
5. If the player can't name the person, the game leader gives one of the other players a chance to name the person. Whoever names the person gets the card.
6. When all of the cards are gone, the players add up the points on their cards. The player with the most cards wins.

Picture Charades

Players communicate through pictures in this game.

MATERIALS:
Index cards
Markers or crayons
Chart paper
Chart stand
Watch or clock with second hand
Paper
Pencil

PLAYERS:
Game leader
6 to 12 players

PREPARATION:
1. Pick categories for the game cards. For example:

Animals	Transportation	Food	Sports
rabbit	school bus	apple	soccer
kangaroo	airplane	spaghetti	football
fox	taxi	ice cream	baseball
brown bear	train	hot dog	tennis
zebra	spaceship	salad	hockey

2. Make playing cards for each category. Write the name of the category on the back of the card and something from that category on the front.
3. Set up the chart on the stand in front of the room.

ACTIVITY:
1. Divide the players into two teams. The first team chooses one member to be the team artist for the first round.
2. The artist picks a category and draws a card from that category's pile.
3. At the game leader's signal, the artist draws pictures on the chart paper that will give the team clues about the object. The artist may use pictures and signals to help the team guess, but the artist may not speak or write any words.
4. The team has three minutes to guess the object. Team members should call out their guesses. If they guess the object within the three minutes, they score 5 points for the team, and another artist from that team gets a turn.
5. If the team cannot guess the object, the next team chooses an artist.
6. The team with the highest score at the end of the game wins.

WORDS IN ACTION

Rhyming Categories

Players guess rhyming pairs within the categories.

MATERIALS:
Index cards
Marker

PLAYERS:
Game leader
3 to 20 players

PREPARATION:
Print a category on each of the index cards. (See the Categories List.)

ACTIVITY:
1. The game leader keeps a copy of the Rhyming Pairs List.
2. The game leader whispers a pair of rhyming words to the first player.
3. The player picks the category cards that will provide the other players with clues to what the rhyming words are. For example: train/transportation, brain/things people use.
4. The other players must guess what the rhyming words are. They ask the first player questions that can be answered yes or no. The questions can be about one or both of the words. For example, a player might ask, "Does the transportation one move faster than a car?" or "Are both of these used daily?"
5. The game leader keeps track of the number of questions asked. If after 10 questions no one has guessed the words, the game leader can give the players a hint.
6. The first player to guess the rhyming pair then takes a turn in front of the group with a new pair of rhyming words.

Rhyming Categories List

Rhyming Pairs

train/brain
mail/sail
four/pour
tree/knee
rug/bug
bread/sled
school/tool
socks/fox
car/jar
cake/rake
feet/sheet
sky/fly
time/dime
ten/hen
blue/glue
snake/lake
log/hog
say/hay
mug/hug
red/bed
comb/Rome
talk/chalk

Categories

transportation
things in the home
things people use
things found outdoors
animals and insects
toys
clothing
appliances
food
things people do
colors
places
numbers

Punctuation Emphasis

Players choose punctuation marks to show the emphasis of each sentence.

MATERIALS:
Index cards
Marker

PLAYERS:
Game leader
5 to 10 players

PREPARATION:
Make a set of punctuation cards for each player. Mark one index card with a period (.), one with a question mark (?), and one with an exclamation point (!).

ACTIVITY:
1. The first player picks a sentence to read aloud. (See the Sentence List.) The player should read the sentence with emphasis (declarative, explanatory, or interrogatory).
2. The other players show their interpretation of the emphasis by holding up their punctuation cards.
3. The game leader counts the number of correct punctuation cards. Each player with a correct card gets 1 point.
4. The game continues, with a new player reading a question.

Sentence List

The towels are wet
The doorbell rang
My Dad loves chicken soup
Mom's car wouldn't start
My friends are mad
When are you going to eat
He did his homework
This is her first time on a roller coaster
Have you ever eaten lime pie
The dogs were walking on the tightrope
Eric loves snow
Cindy is a better runner
It rained for an hour
He looked everywhere
Our game was cancelled
Is that a new dress
It's too strong a tide to swim
The Dolphins have a new quarterback
What time did you leave

Beautiful Mix-Up

In this game, players have to describe beautiful things unfavorably.

MATERIALS:
Index cards
Marker

PLAYERS:
Game leader
5 to 20 players

It's messy. It runs down your hand. It comes in strange flavors.

PREPARATION:
Print words that describe beautiful things on the cards. For example:

vacation	rose	pizza	ice cream
new baby	new penny	sunset	sleigh ride
airplane	puppy	ocean	swan
park	flowers	mountains	swimming hole

ACTIVITY:
1. The game leader shuffles the cards and places the deck facedown.
2. The first player draws the top card and looks at it. The player then must describe the object in a way that makes it sound ugly, unappealing, or unpleasant. For example, to describe a vacation the player might say, "It is too long, it is expensive, and you always get lost." To describe an ice cream cone, the player might say, "It's very messy, it runs down your hand, and it comes in strange flavors."
3. After the player has described the object, the group may ask five questions to try to guess what it is.
4. If no one guesses after the five questions, the game leader names the object and gives the player who described it 5 points.
5. The game continues with a new player describing another object. The player with the most points at the end of the game wins.

Adverb Reaction

In this game, players act out adverbs.

MATERIALS:
Chart paper
Marker

PLAYERS:
Game leader
4 to 20 players

PREPARATION:
Print a list of adverbs on the chart paper.
For example:

easily	restlessly	softly
slowly	coldly	carefully
peacefully	loudly	harshly
quickly	angrily	crisply
rapidly	quietly	lightly
happily	sharply	

Display the chart so that all the players can see it.

ACTIVITY:
1. The game leader picks someone to leave the room.
2. While that player is out, the other players choose one of the adverbs from the list to use as a reaction when the player returns.
3. The player comes back in and tries to guess the adverb by asking questions of each of the other players. The other players respond in a way that gives a clue about the adverb. For example, if the adverb is "softly," the player might say, "Pat, is this a word I would use if I were mad at someone?" Pat would answer by whispering in a soft voice.
4. The questioning continues until the player guesses the adverb. The game leader crosses the adverb off the list and chooses another player to leave the room.

Stump the Leader

Play this game to find a question a friend can't answer.

PLAYERS:
4 to 20 players

ACTIVITY:
1. A player is chosen to be the leader and stands in front of the group. The leader must answer any questions the group asks.
2. Another player asks a question, picking one word that can't be used in the answer. For example, "How old are you? Don't use the word eleven."
3. The leader must answer each question without using the forbidden word. For example, "I'm one year older than I was when I was ten," or "When I celebrate my next birthday, I'll be twelve."
4. The group continues to ask questions, each time specifying a word that can't be used in the answer, until the leader is stumped and can't answer a question.
5. The person who stumped the leader takes over as the leader for the next round.
6. Score the game by counting the number of questions each leader is able to answer before being stumped. The person with the highest number of questions is the winner.

VARIATION:
To make the game more challenging, pick two words that can't be used in the answer. For example, "Where do you go to school? Don't use the words Greenville or school."

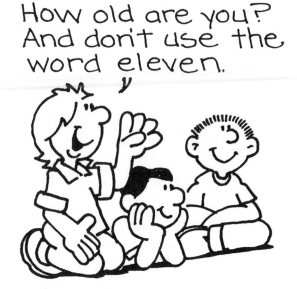

Dare to Do It

Players have to think of new uses for familiar objects.

PLAYERS:
4 to 20 players

ACTIVITY:
1. One player is chosen to be the first leader. The leader thinks of something he or she would like to make. For example, the leader might say, "I would like to make a swimming pool."
2. Another player challenges the leader by naming something that wouldn't normally be used to do it. For example, "I'll bet you can't use a tree branch to make a swimming pool."
3. The leader must give a reasonable way to use the object to do what he or she would like to do. For example, "I could use a tree branch to mark the spot where I want my diving board."
4. When someone stumps the leader, that player takes over as the new leader.
5. Keep score by counting the number of objects named before the leader is stumped. The player with the highest number of objects wins.

Vowel Charades

This version of Charades reinforces familiarity with vowel sounds.

MATERIALS:
Construction paper
Marker or pen
Safety pins

PREPARATION:
Print each of the short and long vowel sounds on a separate sheet of construction paper.

ACTIVITY:
1. The players sit in a circle, and one person is chosen to begin the game. Pin one of the vowel cards on that person's back without letting the person see the card.
2. The player chosen turns around so that everyone can see the vowel sound.
3. The players in the circle think up words that have that vowel sound. The player in the center calls on the people in the circle to act out their words.
4. The player in the middle tries to guess the word and the vowel sound.
5. If the guess is correct, the player who acted out the last word takes a turn in the center.

WORD CHALLENGES

Radio Show

Create a radio show, complete with sound effects.

MATERIALS:
Paper
Pencil
Tape recorder
Tape
Objects for sound effects

PREPARATION:
Make up a story that uses lots of sound effects. (See the sample Radio Show.)

ACTIVITY:
1. Read the story and record it. Leave pauses where sound effects will be added.
2. Collect objects for making sound effects for the story. For example, two blocks of wood can be tapped together for the sound of someone walking up the stairs or a bell used for someone ringing the doorbell.
3. Play the tape, and experiment with the sound effects at the pauses.
4. Play the story for a "radio audience." Have the audience members participate by making the sound effects.

Radio Show: The Baseball Game

Have you ever been to a baseball game? To me, nothing is more exciting. Even now, I can hear the noise of the crowd (*make low throat sounds*) as they wait for the game to start. The first player walks to the plate and taps it with his bat (*tapping sound*). The pitcher winds up and throws the ball. It flies past the batter (*whooshing sound*) and hits the catcher's mitt (*thump*). The umpire calls out (*"Strike one!"*), and the crowd sighs (*sigh*). The batter's heart beats fast (*tap quickly on table*) as he waits for the next pitch. The crowd eagerly awaits it, too. The only sound from the stands is a hot-dog vendor selling hot dogs and peanuts (*"Hot dogs! Peanuts!"*). The batter groans (*groan*) as he swings at the pitch. He makes contact (*hit two pieces of wood together*), and the ball flies high (*whoosh*) to center field! The crowd cries out in amazement (*"Oooh! Aaah!"*) as the ball soars out of the ballpark! The crowd goes wild (*cheers and clapping*)! The home team has won! It seems like only yesterday that I was among those cheering fans at the baseball game.

ABC Game

Try this musical vocabulary challenge.

MATERIALS:
Record or tape
Record player or tape player
Pencils
Writing paper

PLAYERS:
Scorekeeper
Up to 30 players

PREPARATION:
1. Pick a song with clear, understandable words.
2. Have the players write a letter of the alphabet (A through Z) on each line of paper.

ACTIVITY:
1. The scorekeeper starts the record. The players write each word they hear in the song beside the letter that begins the word. Only one word per letter will be counted, but players can write as many words as they want.
2. When the song is over, the players check their lists and count the number of letters they have words for.
3. The scorekeeper checks the scores. The player with the most words wins. In case of a tie, the scorekeeper checks the spellings. The player with the most words that are spelled correctly wins.
4. The winner picks the next song for the players to use.

Souped-Up Words

Use alphabet soup mix to play this game.

MATERIALS:
Dried alphabet soup mix
Sheets of black construction paper
Spoon

PLAYERS:
Scorekeeper
Timekeeper
Up to 20 players

ACTIVITY:
1. Each player gets a sheet of black construction paper. One player is the scorekeeper and one player is the timekeeper.
2. Pour a spoonful of alphabet soup mix onto each player's paper. Players can have a minute to organize their letters.
3. When the timekeeper says "Go," the players have five minutes to try to make as many words as possible from the letters.
4. After five minutes, the timekeeper says "Time." The players then have three minutes to trade their unused letters.
5. The players then have three more minutes to use their new letters to make more words.
6. After three minutes, the timekeeper says "Stop." The players then add up their scores and report them to the scorekeeper. Points are scored as follows:

> two-letter words: 2 points
> three-letter words: 5 points
> four-letter words: 7 points
> five-letter words: 10 points
> six-letter words: 12 points
> seven-letter words: 15 points

7. Keep score for each round of play, and play to 200, 300, or 400 points.

VARIATION:
Make the game more challenging by giving the players less time, not allowing two-letter or three-letter words, or giving extra points for words that use Q, V, X, and Z.

Alphabet Poetry

Use alphabet cereal to create poetry.

MATERIALS:
Colored construction paper
Markers
Dried alphabet cereal
Glue

ACTIVITY:
1. Each player gets five to seven letters from the alphabet cereal.
2. The players arrange their letters vertically on the construction paper in any order. Each letter will begin a new line of a poem. For example, if the player had the letters W, R, B, L, and D, the player might create this poem:

> Beautiful
> Running in the field
> Wild and free
> Leading the young
> Deer

3. When the players have decided the order for the letters, they can glue them onto the paper and write in the rest of the poems with markers.

44

Cause and Effect Toss

Players must stay on their toes to catch a ball and complete a cause-and-effect sentence.

MATERIALS:
Soft rubber ball or sponge

PLAYERS:
6 to 20 players

ACTIVITY:
1. The players sit in a large circle.
2. The first player holds the ball and says the first part of a cause-and-effect sentence. For example:

> When the lights went out . . .
> If Janey misses baseball practice . . .
> Since Gary sold the most boxes of cookies . . .
> When Dad tried to start a fire . . .
> Because her bike was broken . . .

3. The player then tosses the ball to another player in the circle. The player who catches the ball must complete the sentence.
4. If the player completes the sentence, he or she starts a new sentence and tosses the ball to another player. If the player can't complete the sentence or drops the ball, the ball goes back to the person who tossed it. That player restates the beginning of the sentence and tosses the ball to another player in the circle.

Bean Sounds

Use beans to practice beginning, middle, and ending sounds.

MATERIALS:
Index cards
Marker
Three coffee cups
Container of dried beans

PREPARATION:
1. Print "beginning," "middle," and "ending" on three of the index cards.
2. Print vocabulary or spelling words on the other index cards. Underline one letter in each of the words that can be identified as a beginning, middle, or ending sound. For example, if the word is "embarrass," underline the "b" for a middle sound. For "slow," underline the "s" for a beginning sound. For "card," underline the "d" for an ending sound.
3. Place the coffee cups on a table where the players can reach them, and place the "beginning," "middle," and "ending" cards in front of the cups. Set the container of dried beans near the cups.

ACTIVITY:

1. Players work with partners. One player picks a word card and reads it to the other player. The first player then asks the partner where the sound of the underlined letter is heard. For example, "Where do you hear the sound of b?"
2. The second player shows where the sound is heard by putting a bean into the correct cup. For example, if the word is "embarrass" and the underlined letter is "b," the player would put the bean in the cup marked "middle."

Dictionary

Earn points in this game by writing and choosing correct word meanings.

MATERIALS:
Dictionary
Pencils
Paper

PLAYERS:
Game leader
5 to 20 players

ACTIVITY:

1. Players may divide into teams or work individually. A game leader is chosen for each round.

2. The game leader picks an unusual word from the dictionary. The word should be one whose definition most people wouldn't know. The game leader reads the word, but not the definition, aloud to the other players.

3. The players create definitions for the word and write them down. The game leader writes down the correct definition.

4. The game leader collects the definitions and reads them aloud, including the correct definition. The players vote on the definition they think is correct.

5. The game is scored as follows:

   5 points for the player or players who guess correctly

   2 points for a wrong definition

   3 points for having your definition chosen

   10 points for the game leader if nobody guesses the definition

6. The game continues with a new game leader and new word. The player or team with the most points at the end of the game wins.

Headlines

Players match headlines and stories to earn points in this game.

MATERIALS:
Newspaper
Scissors
Glue
Index cards
Library pockets
Poster board
Marker

PREPARATION:
1. Cut short stories from the newspaper that are complete in one column.
2. Cut the headlines from the stories, and glue them on index cards.
3. Glue the library pockets on the poster board in a row, and glue the stories on the pockets.
4. Number the stories and put the corresponding numbers on the back of the index cards for self-checking.

ACTIVITY:
1. Players take turns trying to match headlines with the stories. The player puts the headline card into the story pocket.
2. When the player is through, he or she can check to see if the matches are correct by checking the numbers on the backs of the cards.
3. Players get 1 point for each correct match.

VARIATION:
Make the game more challenging by using longer or more complicated stories.

TEAM GAMES

Comparisons

In this game, players look for something very different things have in common.

MATERIALS:
Paper
Pencils

PLAYERS:
4 to 12 players

ACTIVITY:
1. Divide the players into teams of two or three people. Each team divides a piece of paper into four squares.
2. Each team chooses four categories from the Categories List and prints one at the top of each square.
3. Team members brainstorm things in each category. For example, if one of the categories is food, the team might list banana, spaghetti, roast beef, apple, grapes, and taco. If the category is transportation, the team might list car, truck, train, jet, and skateboard.
4. When the teams have completed their lists, they circle an object in each of their categories. The team then writes these four objects on the back of the paper.
5. The teams trade papers. Each team gets five minutes to think of ways that the two objects are alike. For example, a banana is like a train because they are both long and narrow, both have insides, and both are narrow at one end.
6. The teams should make as many comparisons as possible. If they finish early, the teams can make more comparisons, using the other objects circled.
7. When the time is up, the teams read their comparisons. The teams earn a point for each comparison made.

Categories List

transportation
famous people
tools
clothing
things at the beach
music stars
toys
things associated with school
things a police officer does
things found in a science lab
things that are red
things you see on the highway
foods

holidays
state capitals
things found in a doctor's office
things used to write with
things made from trees
appliances
colors
things found in a kitchen
insects
famous places
favorite books
animals
community helpers

From Here to There

In this game, players name all of the things between opposites

MATERIALS:
Index cards
Marker

PLAYERS:
5 to 12 players

PREPARATION:
Print a pair of opposites on each index card. (See the Opposites List.)

ACTIVITY:
1. The players form a line. The first person in the line draws a card and reads the pair of opposites aloud.
2. The player then names something that would represent one extreme of the opposites. The next player names something that is not as extreme as the first object. The players in line continue to name things until the last player names something that represents the other opposite on the card.
3. The players should be careful to name something that would fit between what the player before said and what the player after might say. For example, for the "tall and short" card, the players might name the following things in order:

>redwood tree
>high diving board
>giraffe
>basketball player
>pony
>fence post
>chair
>poodle

4. After each pair of opposites, the end player moves to the front of the line and draws a new card.

VARIATION:
Play with two teams taking turns drawing cards. Time each round.

Opposites List

tall and short

heavy and light

loud and quiet

hot and cold

wet and dry

dark and light

rough and smooth

dull and shiny

small and large

sweet and sour

sharp and dull

cheap and expensive

funny and serious

low and high

easy and difficult

slow and fast

City Scramble

Teams compete to name cities that begin with the same letter.

MATERIALS:
Oaktag
Marker
Two baskets

PLAYERS:
Game leader
2 scorekeepers
6 to 20 players

PREPARATION:
1. Cut the oaktag into 52 small squares. Make two sets of alphabet cards, printing one letter per card.
2. Place a set of alphabet cards in each basket.

ACTIVITY:
1. Divide into two teams, and pick a scorekeeper for each team.
2. The teams form two lines. The scorekeepers stand about three feet in front of the teams and hold the baskets.
3. When the game leader says "Go," the first player on each team draws a letter from the team's basket without looking.
4. The players read their letters to the scorekeepers and each name a city that begins with the letter drawn.
5. The scorekeepers determine if the city is familiar. If it is, the scorekeeper signals the next player to come draw a card.
6. The teams continue drawing cards and naming cities until each team member has had two turns. The first team to finish is the winner.

VARIATION:
Play the game using states, foods, or famous people instead of cities.

Next Letter Please

This game provides practice in alphabetical order through the use of writing in code.

MATERIALS:
Paper
Pencils

PLAYERS:
8 to 12 players

ACTIVITY:
1. Players form two teams. Each team is given a sheet of paper and a pencil.
2. Beginning at the same time, the first player on each team thinks of a three-letter word. The player then writes the word in code at the top of the paper, using the next letter of the alphabet for each letter of the word. For example, "out" would be written "pvu."
3. The player then passes the paper to the next player on the team. This player must write the correct spelling of the word and then write another three-letter word in code.
4. The paper is passed to each team member, with each one adding a word in code after decoding the previous player's word.
5. The first team to decode all the words correctly wins.
6. To start the game again, have the first player move to the back of the line.

How to Do It

Teams create how-to instructions for familiar activities.

MATERIALS:
Pencils
Paper

PLAYERS:
3 to 21 players

ACTIVITY:
1. Players divide into three teams. The first team picks a familiar chore or activity to describe, such as brushing teeth, getting dressed, making popcorn, or riding a bicycle, and writes a long, wordy description of the steps for the activity. For example, if the chore were brushing teeth, the how-to instructions would provide a long, wordy description of a toothbrush and toothpaste, opening the tube of toothpaste, putting the toothpaste on the toothbrush, brushing up and down, etc.
2. The next team takes the instructions and crosses out as many words as possible, but still leaving enough information in the instructions for someone to be able to do the activity.
3. The third team then picks a member to act out the activity, while the team members try to guess what it is.

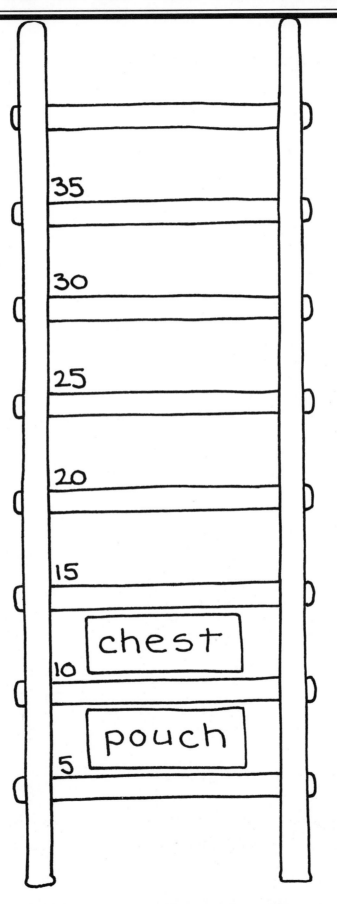

35

30

25

20

15

chest

10

pouch

5

License Plates

Use creative-writing skills to make personalized license plates.

MATERIALS:
Oaktag
Scissors
Markers
Paper
Pencils

PREPARATION:
Cut license plates from the oaktag.

ACTIVITY:
1. Each license plate has seven places for letters or numbers, although some license plates use fewer than seven. Practice writing license plate messages on scrap paper.
2. Use the markers to make license plates on the oaktag.
3. Display the license plates on bicycles, desks, walls, or a bulletin board.

MISSOURI AUG

WERNO 1

SHOW-ME-STATE

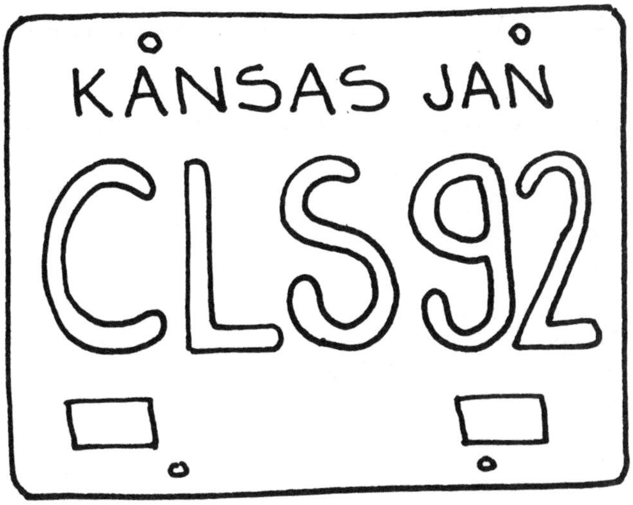

KANSAS JAN

CLS 92

CALIFORNIA APRIL

IOSNE 1

MINNESOTA OCT

CUL8R

LAND OF 10,000 LAKES

GEORGIA JULY

IDRFUL

NEW MEXICO SEPT

CATLVR

Letter Shift

Make new words by changing one letter at a time.

MATERIALS:
Chalkboard
Chalk
Dictionary

PLAYERS:
Game leader
3 to 20 players

ACTIVITY:
1. The leader begins the game by printing a three-letter or four-letter word on the chalkboard.
2. The other players take turns making a new word by changing one letter. The game leader prints the new word under the last word. For example, if the first word is bake, the list might look like this:

     bake
     take
     tale
     tall
     talk
     balk
     back

3. The game leader may consult a dictionary to check spelling or to verify a word.
4. When the players can no longer make a new word, the last player to make a word becomes the new game leader and picks another word for the next round.
5. Keep track of the number of words made on each round, and try to beat the record.

VARIATION:
Play the game with two teams. Each team gets the same word and makes a list of the new words made. The team with the most words wins.

Prefix and Suffix Flip Book

Make new words by flipping the prefix and suffix cards.

MATERIALS:
Oaktag
Scissors
Marker
Book rings
Hole punch
Pencils
Paper
Dictionary

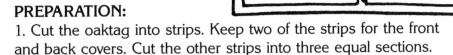

PREPARATION:
1. Cut the oaktag into strips. Keep two of the strips for the front and back covers. Cut the other strips into three equal sections.
2. Print root words, prefixes, and suffixes on the cards. (See the Word List.)
3. Put the root words in a pile, and punch a hole through the top of the cards. Do the same thing for the prefixes and for the suffixes.
4. Attach each set with a book ring.
5. Make three holes in the front and back covers. Complete the book by attaching the covers with the rings.

ACTIVITY:
1. Players work individually to form as many words as they can by flipping the prefixes, suffixes, and root words. Players record the words that they have formed.
2. When each player has had a turn, the players trade lists and check the words in a dictionary to make sure the words are correct.

Word List

Prefixes	Base Words	Suffixes
pre	cord	ed
mis	order	ant
in	color	er
re	test	ly
uni	form	able
con	vent	s
un	wash	ing
dis	lead	less

Picture Puzzles

This game tests visual memory.

MATERIALS:
Magazines
Scissors
Construction paper
Glue
Watch or clock with a second hand
Pencils
Paper

PLAYERS:
Timekeeper
2 to 30 players

ACTIVITY:
1. Each player gets a magazine, scissors, construction paper, and glue. The players cut pictures out of the magazines and glue them on the construction paper. The players should write their names on the back on the construction paper.
2. When all of the picture puzzles are completed, the timekeeper collects the puzzles. The timekeeper then puts someone else's puzzle facedown in front of each player.
3. When the timekeeper gives the signal, the players turn the puzzles over and look at them carefully for one minute.
4. When the timekeeper says stop, the players turn the puzzles facedown again.
5. The players then have three minutes to write down everything they remember seeing on the puzzles.
6. After three minutes are up, the players give the puzzles back to the people who made them, along with the lists to be checked.
7. The player with the most correct answers is the winner.

Comic Strip Stories

Create new stories by combining comic strips.

MATERIALS:
Newspaper comic strips
Index cards
Rubber cement

PREPARATION:
1. Collect as many comic strips from newspapers as possible.
2. Cut the panels of the comic strips apart.
3. Glue each panel on an index card.
4. Shuffle the cards, and place the deck facedown.

ACTIVITY:
1. Each player draws six cards.
2. The players then put the cards together to create a new comic strip story.
3. Points are awarded as follows:
    Use 6 frames: 6 points
    Use 5 frames: 4 points
    Use 4 frames: 3 points
    Use 2 frames: 1 point
4. Return the cards to the deck and shuffle them for the next round. After each round, the players vote for the most original comic strip story. The winner gets an additional 5 points.
5. Play three rounds, add up each player's points, and declare a winner.
6. Add new comic strips to the collection for future games.

Vocabulary Ladder

Use this game to practice vocabulary words.

MATERIALS:
Index cards
Marker
Poster board

PLAYERS:
Game leader
2 to 10 players

PREPARATION:
1. Print vocabulary words on the index cards.
2. Draw a ladder on the poster board. Leave room between each step of the ladder for an index card.
3. Print a score next to each step of the ladder, starting with 5 for the lowest step and continuing in multiples of 5.

ACTIVITY:
1. The game leader shuffles the cards, and places the deck facedown.
2. Each player takes a turn drawing a card, reading the word aloud, and giving a definition for the word.
3. The game leader decides if the definition is correct. If it is, the word card is placed on the first step. The player draws another card and defines the word. The player moves up another step for each correct definition.
4. When the player reaches the top or cannot define a word, the game leader counts up the player's score for each step, and another player takes a turn.
5. The winner is the player who has the highest score after all the players have had a turn. The winner is the game leader for the next round. If there is a tie, the last player to reach the top of the ladder is the next game leader.